How to Exasperate Your Wife
& Other Short Essays for Men

Published by Canon Press
P.O. Box 8729, Moscow, Idaho 83843
800.488.2034 | www.canonpress.com

Douglas Wilson, *How to Exasperate Your Wife and Other Short Essays for Men*
Copyright ©2015 by Douglas Wilson.

Cover and interior design by James Engerbretson.
Cover illustration by Forrest Dickison.
Interior layout by Valerie Anne Bost.

Printed in the United States of America.

Library of Congress Cataloging-in-Publication Data is forthcoming.

22 23 24 25   12 11 10 9 8 7 6 5 4 3

How to Exasperate Your Wife

& Other Short Essays for Men

DOUGLAS WILSON

canonpress
Moscow, Idaho

This book is for Christian wives everywhere.
Thanks for being such good sports.

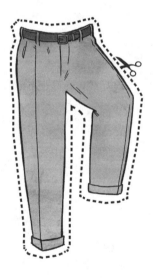

FREE PANTS
for the caveman on the cover

TABLE OF CONTENTS

THE MEANING
OF HONOR

CHAPTER 1

WISDOM IS A WOMAN

T he apostle Peter tells husbands to live with their wives with knowledge. But many modern men face a barrier when they consider these words. They do not understand women because they do not understand wisdom, and they do not understand wisdom because they do not approach her as a woman.

Throughout the book of Proverbs—a book for teaching wisdom to young men—wisdom appears as a *woman*. The book begins with two women, personifications of wisdom and folly respectively, and it ends with a particular woman. As a woman, wisdom appears under various aspects, and men who would be wise must approach her with all these separate aspects in mind. While some of the feminine aspects of wisdom are not *directly* applicable to a man's understanding of his wife, several are.

First, she is an instructor, a teacher, and a schoolmarm ready to rap our knuckles (Prov. 1:20–25), hauling us out of the classroom by the ear. Wisdom is a woman who effectively teaches little-boy-simpletons. This means that a man who pursues wisdom should make it one of his life's pursuits to seek, among other things, to sit still in his desk and try to keep ink off his face. Wisdom is pursued with humility.

Wisdom is also a wealthy patroness, one who throws spectacular banquets to which we are wonderfully invited. "Wisdom hath builded her house, she hath hewn out her seven pillars: She hath killed her beasts; she hath mingled her wine; she hath also furnished her table" (Prov. 9:1–2). A man who pursues wisdom should behave as a man behaves who is invited to dine at a palace or mansion. He should respond to the invitation, watch his manners, and eat what is served, all the while rejoicing in the wisdom that comes with bread and wine. Wisdom is pursued with gladness and joy; wisdom is gained with a knife and fork.

While all this is important, the remaining aspects of feminine wisdom are more directly relevant to the man who wants to pursue wisdom as a means of learning how to dwell together with his wife.

Wisdom is a sexually attractive woman (Prov. 7:4) and should be sought as any sensible suitor would court a beautiful and intelligent woman. The name *sister* in this context should be taken the same way it is taken in the Song of Songs (Song 5:1). The man who passionately courts wisdom here is protected in the next verse from the "strange woman," who flatters with her words. When wisdom is *courted*, seduction loses its allure. When the feminine personification of wisdom is courted, a man is protected from very tangible, non-personified hookers and tramps. When men come to see wisdom as altogether lovely, and they seek to win *her* hand, they are sexually protected.

A wise man marries this woman and is instructed to be faithful to her. She is a dear wife, never to be forsaken. "Get wisdom, get understanding: forget it not; neither decline from the words of my mouth. Forsake *her* not, and *she* shall preserve thee: love *her*, and *she* shall keep thee" (Prov. 4:5–6). This is the language of marriage. A man who ditches the actual wife of his youth is thereby revealing that he abandoned another woman (Wisdom) some time before. Before he leaves his wife for some young twinkie with enhanced mammaries, he has to have already left wisdom for folly.

Wisdom is our mother, and speaks to us as to her children. "Now therefore hearken unto me, O ye children: for blessed are they that keep my ways. Hear instruction, and be wise, and refuse it not" (Prov. 8:32–33). In this image, wisdom is *our* mother, but viewing wisdom as a mother enables a man to see his wife *as a mother* as well, and this teaches him to respect her high calling.

This approach to wisdom—treating her as a woman—collides sharply with the approach of modernity, which sees wisdom as a pile of rocks. These rocks are to be sorted out, counted, and organized into smaller piles according to size, color, and weight. The world is thought to be a place of brute facts, all needing to be fashioned into a more efficient ball-bearing factory. The ancient word says that wisdom is a woman to be approached with a rose, a sonnet, or both; we think it is a mountain to be razed with strip-mining equipment.

When it comes to obeying Peter's injunction to live with our wives with knowledge, men of all ages have unfortunately been dense. But modern men have this additional handicap: we have a false understanding of wisdom that distorts how we understand most of the world around us. It is little wonder that we don't understand our wives.

CHAPTER 2

THE CROWN OF HER HUSBAND

When Scripture teaches that a wife is the crown of her husband, far more is involved than the idea that a wife is a decorative add-on. The apostle teaches us that woman is the glory of man, and teaches us further that this is a great mystery. Anyone who believes he has the concept down pat is simply demonstrating that he doesn't have the faintest idea.

As always, the ultimate pattern of this is Christ and the Church. If a woman is the crown of her husband, then the ultimate example of this is the Church considered as the crown of Christ. And this is exactly what we find Paul teaching us throughout the book of Ephesians. When he gets to the famous section on marriage in chapter five, he is *not* introducing a new subject.

The glory brought to Christ by the Church is not an incidental glory. The greatness of grace can be seen through how much God actually does in the mystery of redemption. Paul tells us in the first chapter that *all* things in heaven and on earth are brought together in Christ and united in Him (Eph. 1:10). The marriage of Christ to His bride has cosmic significance.

After his resurrection, Jesus Christ was granted universal dominion far above "all principality, and power, and might, and dominion, and every name that is named, not only in this world, but also in that which is to come" (1:21). Notice too that God has placed all things under His feet and "gave him to be the head over all things *to the church*" (1:22). In plain language, Christ owns everything in heaven and on earth, and this wealth has ramifications for His wife. What He owns, *she* owns.

She in turn is His body, "the fulness of him that filleth all in all" (1:23). The Church is married to the one who fills the universe, *and she fills Him.* How is this possible? A woman is the crown of her husband, and not only is it no different with Christ and the Church, it is preeminently true with Christ and the Church.

Obviously, this is only possible by the infinite grace of the omnipotent God, and even with that proviso, seeing how it could happen is difficult. But Paul, like Moses, is hungry for glory, so long as it is the glory of the only wise God. He prays that the Ephesians would be given this same hunger to know the glory of the Church.

> That Christ may dwell in your hearts by faith; that ye, be-
> ing rooted and grounded in love, may be able to compre-
> hend with all saints what is the breadth, and length, and
> depth, and height; and to know the love of Christ, which
> passeth knowledge, that ye might be filled with all the ful-
> ness of God. Now unto him that is able to do exceeding
> abundantly above all that we ask or think, according to the
> power that worketh in us, *unto him be glory in the church*
> by Christ Jesus throughout all ages, world without end.
> Amen. (Eph. 3:17–21)

Paul prays that they would come to know the unknowable. He wants them to grasp the ungraspable, to pick up
the infinite. He wants them to be filled with all the fullness
of God, which is like getting the Pacific Ocean into a coffee
cup. "Filled with all the fulness of God"—this is how we can
be the fullness of Christ who fills everything in every way.
God fills us with His fullness by grace through faith, and we
are made the fullness of Christ.

But these superlative statements are still insufficient
for Paul. He goes on to say that God is able to do exceed-
ing abundantly beyond all this, beyond what we can ask
or think. But whatever He does, it will be according to
the power at work within us; it will be glory to Him *in the
Church*. This is all possible because we are a habitation of
God through the Spirit (2:22).

When Christ first made His choice of a bride evident, it
was the ultimate case of bystanders thinking that it was a
crazy choice. But God had a greater purpose in mind, and
He had this purpose in mind from before the foundation of

the world. He wanted to show the principalities and powers the manifold nature of His wisdom, and He wanted to do it *by the Church* (Eph. 3:9–10).

So when Paul begins teaching on marriage in chapter five, he is not changing the subject. Rather, he is assuming that the husbands have been listening to his teaching on the Church, and they want to know the unknowable, and they want to manifest the glory of Christ's bride throughout heaven and earth. How are husbands to make this declaration? They are to show that they understand this doctrine through how they treat their own wives. Show what kind of crown the Church is to Christ by making your own wife your glory, your honor, and your crown.

Husbands, do what Christ did and you will have what Christ has—a glorious crown:

> Husbands, love your wives, even as Christ also loved the church, and gave himself for it; that he might sanctify and cleanse it with the washing of water by the word, that he might present it to himself a glorious church, not having spot, or wrinkle, or any such thing; but that it should be holy and without blemish. (Eph. 5:25–27)

This is far more than what can be attained at a marriage enrichment seminar. "This is a great mystery: but I speak concerning Christ and the church" (Eph. 5:32).

CHAPTER 3

THE WIFE AS RULER

In a biblical home, the wife has far more practical authority than some reactionary Christians might suppose. Biblical thinking on role relationships between men and women requires more than simply offending the feminists. Since this is so easily done, such a standard is far too low. We have to look more closely at what the Scriptures actually teach.

As the apostle Paul is urging young women to marry, he lets a very interesting comment fall in passing. "I will therefore that the younger women marry, bear children, *guide the house*, give none occasion to the adversary to speak reproachfully" (1 Tim. 5:14). The word translated here as "guide the house" is *oikodespotein*. The wife is to be the ruler or *despot* of the home. This means that when she tells you to take your shoes off at the door, you *will* take your shoes off—and cheerfully.

This does not contradict what the Bible teaches else-where about the husband's authority and headship. In the family, the husband is the head of his wife, as Christ is the head of the church. He is also the head of the home and has the responsibility to protect and provide for that household. He is responsible to lead and he has the authority to do so.

But wise leadership never micro-manages and never in-sists upon the prerogative of making all decisions that have to be made. To take an example from elsewhere, the busi-ness world is filled with failures who were undone because they were highly competent control freaks. In contrast to this, a good leader in business is one who finds or cultivates competent men to whom he can delegate responsibility.

Something similar happens in marriage. A man should marry a woman *whom he can trust*: "The heart of her hus-band doth safely trust in her . . ." (Prov. 31:11). But trust defined in the context of marriage is not simply believing that she will do well if any problem ever comes up, and it involves far more than thinking she will not go out honky-tonkin'. Trust here means *en*trusting, and something has to be there to be entrusted. In a godly home, that which is entrusted is the management of the home and all the in-habitants thereof.

Of course, the husband is not "under" her command—she ought not to boss him around like he is one of the kids—but at the same time, he is called upon to honor the standards which she establishes for the home. This will en-sure that everyone in the house will see that he honors and respects her judgments. He married her; he *entrusted* these things to her. In respecting her judgments, he is standing by his own judgment.

So let's make it practical. Let's say Mom wants everyone to wash up in the mudroom and not in the kitchen. She wants them to put their dirty clothes in the laundry room as opposed to their ongoing attempts to make a compost pile out of them in the back of the closet. She wants everybody's "stuff" to find its way away from the pile at the front door. She wants shod feet off the couch. She wants plates rinsed and put in the dishwasher. All these desires have the force of law, and everyone, including her husband, should honor them. In a very real way, the home is her domain. She is not the head of the home, but she is the executive of it.

If her wishes are routinely disregarded, this means that her husband has failed to invest her with his authority, and has failed to act as an example for the rest of the household. A sure indicator of an unhappy household is the ignoring of Mom, and the head of *that* home is an abdicating father.

Another great blessing arises from wives seeing their authority in this. Authority, known to be such, is more carefully wielded than kibitzing is wielded. If a woman sees her desires being implemented as a simple question of raw competition, survival of the fittest, and devil take the hindmost, she will be tempted to nag, and nagging is frequently irrational and contradictory. But if she knows that her word is law with regard to the management of the home, then she will be more careful about what she requires.

None of this means that she is chained to the home; rather, she is within her element there. It is the domain in which she is gifted by God to bear authority. This is not her burden to bear any more than birds are troubled by having to haul their wings around.

CHAPTER 4

AN HONORED GUEST

The headship that God grants the husband in marriage is widely discussed, but it is not widely understood. Often both sides of the debate, whether traditionalist or feminist, share the same misunderstanding. Their differences arise because one group embraces the misunderstanding while the other rejects it.

Unfortunately, many conservative husbands do not grasp the organic nature of their authority in the home. They have read that the husband is the head of the wife, but they then fill this language with connotations derived elsewhere—from their stint in the Army, from the shift manager at work, or from the leadership techniques of Tamerlane. In short, they think that head of the wife means *boss* of the wife, end of discussion, and where's my supper? Or sex, as the case may be.

In referring to the organic nature of authority in the home, I mean that true scriptural authority is living, supple, and complicated. Secular denials or counterfeits of this tend to be simple and rigid. Egalitarian feminism is simple to understand, and because of this, it has all the subtlety of a wooden fence. It has no way of accounting for how men and women actually *are*. By the same token, masculinist domineering is equally simplistic. Perhaps the nature of these two positions can be seen through a comparison to their political counterparts. Feminism is like strict democracy—a flat horizontal line. Masculinism is like a divine-right-of-kings monarchy—a straight vertical line.

But a biblical marriage is more like the lines of a complex Celtic design. It is like a feudal monarchy, with the monarch having true authority in his assigned realm, but with the vassals having a different but equally true authority in their respective realms. In feudalism, those in authority owe certain things to those they are responsible for, and those under authority have the right to demand those things. Those under authority owe certain things to their liege-lord, and the one in authority has the right to require it of them. But all the persons involved in this are equally bound in an organic, constitutional way. No one person is absolute.

And this is why those husbands who think that headship means their wives should never offer a contrary view are wrong. This is why husbands who think their wives cannot require certain things of them are wrong. This is why husbands who believe that their wives have no court of appeal outside the marriage are wrong.

The husband delegates responsibilities to his wife, but he does so as an instrument of the already established scriptural constitution of the home. In other words, he must delegate to her what the Scripture requires. He may not delegate to her a responsibility which Scripture has assigned to *him*. An example of the former would be a delegation of the responsibility to manage the home. An example of the latter would be an abdication of his responsibility to go to war to defend his household, making her go instead.

Paul teaches this principle clearly: "I will therefore that the younger women marry, bear children, guide the house, give none occasion to the adversary to speak reproachfully" (1 Tim. 5:14). As I have noted before, the phrase "guide the house" is a translation of one Greek word which could be literally rendered as "house-despot." The wife is the mistress of this domain; this is assigned to her by God. The husband can (and must) delegate this complex web of responsibilities to her. He has no right to withhold such a delegation.

Paul says something similar elsewhere. "That they may teach the young women to be sober, to love their husbands, to love their children, to be discreet, chaste, keepers at home, good, obedient to their own husbands, that the word of God be not blasphemed (Titus 2:4–5). "Keepers at home" renders one word which would literally be "house-guard." A wife therefore has true authority over her home which no one, including her husband, can take away from her. She must be obedient to him, as this verse states, but this is a clearly delimited obedience.

This can easily be misunderstood or misrepresented, but it is still necessary to emphasize. In a certain sense, a husband (as the head of his wife) is an honored and permanent guest, but he should learn to see himself *as a guest*. He wipes his feet at the door, he eats what is served to him, and he seeks to conform to the pattern established by her—as she in her turn seeks to honor him.

He has authority—where Scripture gives it. She has authority where Scripture gives it. In a Christian marriage, Christ is the Lord of it. As Lord, He has assigned these realms of authority to each. Relating these authorities to one another is a complicated dance requiring grace, humility, and love from all the dancers. This means that in certain areas in the life of the home a godly husband is active and engaged. In others, he is to delegate and get out of the way. In yet others, he is to delegate and then do as he is told. But as in everything that Christians do, such "telling" is to be done with grace. A peevish wife is no more scriptural than a cantankerous husband.

A wife has authority over her husband's sex life (1 Cor. 7:4). She has authority over his food (Prov. 31:14). She is responsible for his clothing (Prov. 31:21). (She *is* supposed to stay out of his fishing gear though.)

Is the husband the head of his wife the way Christ is the head of the Church? Absolutely. Is he the boss man? Not even close.

CHAPTER 5

ROMANCE AND THE STORY

O ne of the great mistakes our culture has made in the matter of stories is that we have assumed that detachment from imitation is a duty. We think we are supposed to learn how to enjoy a story "for its own sake," and so we try to suppress our natural inclination to copy what we see and read. Given how God made the world, such attempts are not even remotely successful, but they do accomplish something else—giving people a distaste for imitating nobility, followed by a false confidence that they are not being dragged down by the rest.

Scripture shows us in countless places that we learn by imitation. But we have come to assume that *we* can rise above all that. People who injure themselves trying to imitate stunts they saw in some movie are assumed to be morons, pure and simple, and although their wisdom is certainly lacking, our rude dismissal leaves out something important. Their problem was not that they imitated what they saw, but rather that they saw the wrong thing. Those who seek to maintain a disconnect between the stories they hear, read, and see and the stories they live are in a graver danger.

What does this have to do with husbands? The central command delivered to husbands (considered as such) in the Scriptures is the command to imitate the ultimate story. Because we do not understand "story," we turn the command to love our wives as Christ loved the Church into a statement that Jesus loved His bride "a lot" and so should we. But this is not what it says. Husbands are told to love their wives as Christ loved the Church and gave Himself up for her. How did He do that?

When Adam rejected the goodness of God in the garden, he did so because his wife had been deceived by a lying worm. This worm, this serpent, was a fallen seraph, what we would call a dragon (Gen. 3:1; Num. 21:8–9; Rom. 16:20; Rev. 12:9). But God promised that worm that the seed of the woman and the brood of vipers would be in a constant state of war from that point on. He promised further that a great Prince would come from the seed of the woman and finally and completely crush the head of the serpent. He would Himself be grievously wounded in the conquest, but that conquest would nevertheless come to pass. Sound familiar? A bit fairy-tale-ish? Husbands, love your wives *that* way. A husband who is not imitating the Worm-killer is not really doing what he was told.

But modern husbands don't want to do this. It sounds like it has a large junior-high dorky quotient in it. Husbands would rather love their wives "a lot"—flowers on the anniversary, card on Mother's Day, nice birthday present, come home every night, that sort of thing. It may be a little boring in a suburban kind of way, but hey—it's what we know. What this misses is the scriptural command to live romantically with your wife.

But this is susceptible of misunderstanding. Biblically speaking, the romance of marriage has far more in common with *Beowulf* and the *Song of Roland* than it does with *Love's Breathless Passion* at a Safeway near you. This is because the former are part of a long story-telling tradition that goes back to the opening pages of Genesis. The latter is pornography for the emotions.

Just as husbands are commanded to imitate the Savior, so they should also imitate saviors. These lesser saviors must be understood scripturally—men who laid down or risked their lives in the way of Christ-like sacrifice. And this means that husbands should *learn* from Tirian, King Lune, Aragorn, Beowulf, Robert E. Lee, Alfred the Great, Samwise Gamgee, Roland, Antipas, Polycarp, Jim Eliot, Hugh Latimer, Sam Adams, Ransom, Bonhoeffer, and Athanasius.

We react against this in different ways and for different reasons. Some think that a long chain of names like that is some sort of highbrow elitist roster of names, and that some ordinary Joe shouldn't be required to get a master's degree in history or literature in order to be able to love his wife . . . right? Right, but this overlooks something. Over the centuries, the people who have kept the names of such great men alive have been the common people, not academics with pinched faces. One of the great tragedies of our era is how folk history and literature have been overthrown by the sitcom. My point was that husbands should imitate and learn from such stories, but this is not the same thing as getting the form of the stories from the Trained Professionals. It is better to learn about Robin Hood from the people than from the historians—there are far more valuable lessons there.

What should a husband imitate? The central thing is to learn what an immense array of sacrificial options present themselves to a man who would love his wife in a fallen world, in a world where there are dragons and giants. He can sacrifice his life. Or his wealth. Or his reputation. Or his family. Or his nation. This is because love takes many different forms, according to the lines of the story. And since a man does not know beforehand how *his* story will go, he should have some awareness of how nobility behaves according to the situation.

This is hard for us to grasp. We need the stories.

CHAPTER 6

WHEN A MAN
LOVES A WOMAN

The apostle Paul reminds husbands to love their wives as Christ loved the church. He tells wives in their turn to reverence their husbands, to respect them. When men get this garbled and backwards, one of the results is that they spend their time wondering why their wives don't respect and honor them. And so they start to demand it, making it even less likely that it will ever happen. Few forms of behavior are less respectable than that of demanding to be respected.

When a husband does what Scripture tells him to do, the result is that his wife is washed with the water of the word. He loves her, as Christ loved the church, and one of the blessings that flows from this is the fact that his wife finds herself naturally respecting him. He who loves his wife, Paul says, loves himself. A man who *gives* love *receives* respect.

But marriage is not a vending machine, and love is not two quarters to put into it. This is a manner of life, not an exchange of commodities. So what does this kind of life look like? What does it look like when a man loves a woman?

First, the love that Christ modeled for Christian men was a *particular* love. Another way of putting this is that Christ is monogamous. He gave Himself for His bride, the Church. He has one Church, one bride, one wife. Other worldviews, other religions, and other patterns of philosophy are *not* loved by Him redemptively. Christian men are therefore to be dedicated to one particular woman. Temptations to look aside, to the right or to the left, are temptations to represent Christ and the Church sinfully. Husbands are a walking typology of the gospel, and when they waver in their sexual dedication to their wives, they have begun to model a religious relativism. Lusting after another woman is like saying that Buddhism or Islam has its good points. The particularity of the atonement is very important, but we should never trust a man who affirms this without being equally devoted to his wife. He should treat her like the elect—because typologically that is what she is.

Second, Christ loved His bride *sacrificially* to the point of death, and His perfect, sinless life up to the point of death was an expression of His love for His wife as well. If a man has to literally lay down his life for his wife, it will not be a spasmodic, final event inconsistent with what has gone before. A sacrificial death is unlikely outside the context of a sacrificial life—we do not become suddenly, miraculously obedient at the last minute. If a man has to die for his wife, it ought to be the next logical step. So when Christ gave Himself up for His wife, this sacrifice was characteristic of His entire life. It began in history with the Incarnation, continued through to His baptism, and culminated in His death and resurrection. Too many husbands want the perks of headship in the home ("with dominion, glory and a kingdom, that the wife, sons and daughters, dog and cat, and TV remote should serve him") without understanding that biblical authority in the home is based on sacrifice. The universal dominion of Christ is based squarely on the fact that He died in obedience to the Father. All men who want to be the boss in their home without an ethos of self-sacrifice driving their daily decisions are men who secretly want to be Muslims. But Christian men show honor to their wives by imitating the kind of authority that Jesus modeled, which is the authority of the servant's heart.

Third, a man loves a woman *sacramentally*. She is bone of his bone, flesh of his flesh. This happens when the marriage is consummated on their wedding night, but it is constantly renewed in their sexual life together. This is not a mere physical action, a biological phenomenon. Most contemporary Christians unwittingly set the stage for marital infidelity by how they view the sacraments of the Church. If the Lord's Supper is a "mere" memorial, then eating at the table of devils is "merely" something else. If lovemaking is merely physical, then what does it matter what other physical bodies might get involved? At the other extreme is a mistake that mirrors the Roman Catholic error of the Mass. A couple who become one flesh are not mystically and magically united forever and ever. The sacraments are sacraments of the new covenant; they are covenantal realities. A man loves a woman by maintaining his relations with her, knowing that covenants define relations between persons and that the stipulations of the covenant can be nourished and maintained, or starved and broken.

And last, when a man loves a woman, he does so in a story. Paul says that men are to treat their wives with a certain end in view. In this passage, men are commanded to nourish, cherish, sanctify, cleanse, and present their wives. Nothing about marriage is static—a marriage travels through time. It has characters, development, a plot, and so on. This means that men are responsible to see themselves accurately.

Men can do this by asking the right question. If this household of his were a story (the kind you get from a book), what kind of character would he be in it? The question can bring remarkable and unsettling perspective. Is he the antagonist? The protagonist? The villain? The buffoon? The sidekick? Is this story going to end the way Paul describes in the fifth chapter of Ephesians—"without spot or wrinkle, or any other blemish"? If not, which character is preventing this?

THE MEANING
OF THOUGHTFULNESS

CHAPTER 7

THE TEN COMMANDMENTS IN MARRIAGE

M any of us are accustomed to seeing those "ten commandments" of this and that which show up in sundry places and are applied to all sorts of human endeavors. From closing real estate deals to bagging a trophy elk, we like to mimic the Decalogue. So some may have been lured into this chapter hoping to find a "commandment three" which prohibits the practice of leaving dirty socks draped over the back of the living room couch—sort of like a masculine doily—or "commandment seven" which requires a weekly date.

This chapter, though, is not about the ten commandments *of* marriage. We need to consider the far more important subject of the ten commandments *in* marriage. The Bible teaches us that in terms of its content, love is always defined by the law (Rom. 13: 8–10). Since love clearly should be resident in every believing home, in every Christian marriage, this means that the law should always be seen as love's beautiful twin sister, the two of them never separated.

"Thou shalt have no other gods before me" (Exod. 20:3). A husband must love his wife *less* than he loves God. When a man loves God as he ought, it enables him to love others as he should. But when a woman becomes an idol, she will frequently find herself regularly mistreated in that relationship. This is because the man who idolizes her has, in that attitude, cut himself off from the source of all genuine charity and grace, which is of course the Father. "If any man come to me, and hate not his father, and mother, and wife, and children, and brethren, and sisters, yea, and his own life also, he cannot be my disciple" (Lk. 14:26). A man cannot be a disciple of Christ unless he hates his wife, and unless he is a disciple of Christ, he cannot learn to love his wife.

"Thou shalt not make unto thee any graven image . . . and shewing mercy unto thousands of them that love me, and keep my commandments" (Exod. 20:4a, 6). This commandment mentions the fruit of marriage, counted in the coming generations. One sure way to visit grief upon those children yet unborn is to tolerate any man-made conceptions and images of God and Christ in the name of maintaining a "pious" home.

"Thou shalt not take the name of the LORD thy God in vain; for the LORD will not hold him guiltless that taketh his name in vain" (v. 7). We bear the name of Christ in all that we do. If we are Christians, then our marriages are Christian marriages. But modern evangelical marriages are barely distinguishable from unbelieving marriages. We display the same evidence of pathological disease in our marriages that are seen in the world—widespread divorce, rampant counseling, preoccupation with *our* marital needs, sex-on-the-brain, and so forth. We therefore bear the name of God in vain. Until we learn what the word *Christian* means, we will not do well in understanding what Christian marriage is.

"Remember the sabbath day, to keep it holy. Six days shalt thou labour, and do all thy work: But the seventh day is the sabbath of the Lord thy God" (vv. 8–10a). The frenetic pace of our modern culture is subsidized by husbands who have forgotten that they have a duty to give rest to every member of the household and to do so in the presence of God. In particular, a husband should see to it that the proverb "A woman's work is never done" is false in his household. Anyone in authority who does not give sabbaths does not know what love is.

"Honour thy father and thy mother: that thy days may be long upon the land which the Lord thy God giveth thee" (v. 12). Parents like to receive honor, but parents frequently forget that they also are children, and they are to set an example to their children through how they treat the children's grandparents. Many children have learned how to disrespect parents from simply hearing the conversation at the dinner table. And little pitchers have big ears.

"Thou shalt not kill" (v. 13). The antithesis of the malice that ends in bloodshed is the demeanor of warmth and kindness. A man who loves his wife as Christ loved the church is demonstrating his hatred of all lawless bloodshed.

"Thou shalt not commit adultery" (v. 14). Of course, a husband obeys God here by avoiding infidelity in all its guises and forms. He sets a guard over his eyes, heart, and his members which are on the earth, and refuses all offers. He turns away from the covers of magazines at the supermarket checkout, he stays out of conversations with women in Internet chat rooms, he stays out of bed with other women, he refuses to daydream about being married to someone else, and any other similar temptation.

"Thou shalt not steal" (v. 15). A man who does not provide food and clothing for his wife is robbing her. He owes her financial support and must never begrudge it.

"Thou shalt not bear false witness against thy neighbour" (v. 16). A man's wife is his closest neighbor. He therefore must be scrupulously honest with her at all times. A man and wife should be able to talk with one another about anything.

"Thou shalt not covet thy neighbour's house, thou shalt not covet thy neighbour's wife, nor his manservant, nor his maidservant, nor his ox, nor his ass, nor any thing that is thy neighbour's" (v. 17). A happily married man will never spend any time looking longingly over the fence at anything. He may not covet the lawnmower over there, the wife sunbathing, the car, the house itself, the driveway, the gardening ability, or anything else belonging to his neighbor.

Do this, and you do well.

CHAPTER 8

TRY A LITTLE TENDERNESS

—————

I t may have been a lousy book—I don't know—but it did have a great title. Somewhere, many years ago, I saw a book entitled *The Velvet Covered Brick* and thought it expressed a profound biblical truth wonderfully. A husband must be hard in order to take on masculine responsibility. A husband must be soft in order to avoid crushing those for whom he is responsible. Maintaining these twin imperatives in balance requires great wisdom, far more than men may have apart from the grace of God.

Some men are all velvet—the kind Christ contemptuously dismissed as fit only for a life in politics. "But what went ye out for to see? A man clothed in soft raiment? Behold, they that wear soft clothing are in kings' houses" (Mt. 11:8). Other men are all brick, mostly between the ears. "Now the name of the man was Nabal; and the name

33

of his wife Abigail: and she was a woman of good under-standing, and of a beautiful countenance: but the man was churlish and evil in his doings; and he was of the house of Caleb" (1 Sam. 25:3).

Other men prefer to alternate between the two. Bricks when angry and abdicating velvet when covenantally lazy, they manage to incur all the negative consequences of *both* kinds of sin. This is the kind of husband whose wife thinks he is a tyrant, although he has never made one clear deci-sion in all their years together.

The Bible says that a husband must not be harsh or bitter with his wife (Col. 3:19). At the same time, the husband must provide godly strength and leadership. "Therefore as the church is subject unto Christ, so let the wives be to their own husbands in every thing" (Eph. 5:24). The problem is how to be hard enough to lead, and soft enough . . . to lead.

Peter instructs husbands in this difficult art of marital wis-dom. "Likewise, ye husbands, dwell with them according to knowledge, giving honour unto the wife, as unto the weaker vessel, and as being heirs together of the grace of life; that your prayers be not hindered" (1 Pet. 3:7). A husband with understanding—one who dwells with his wife "according to knowledge"—is a husband who *honors* his wife as a weak-er vessel. Both elements are here—his strength over against her weakness, and his honor of her equality with him as a fellow Christian, an heir of grace together with him. And this brings us to our point, which is that a man cannot hon-or a woman unless he is tender with her. A man cannot be an obedient husband unless he honors and respects his wife. But this is not what fawning courtiers can do, or what the Nabals of this world want to do.

The Bible tells men to be hard, and it tells them to be soft. Around each command, we find men clustering according to their own wishes and desires. One husband hears loud and clear the command to be hard, and so he engages himself to be harsh, critical, unloving, dense, imperious, stubborn, unbending, idiotic, and proud. Another man hears the command to be soft, and so he vacillates, waffles, abdicates, whines, complains, suffers, agonizes, and goes generally limp.

A man who does the former does so in the name of strength but has no notion of what biblical strength really is. A man who does the latter does so in the name of kindness but has no idea what biblical kindness actually is.

A man who is not strong enough to be tender is not strong at all. Everything he projects is nothing but counterfeit bluster. This is easy for us to miss. For example, we like to think that Pharisees were excessively righteous, but this was not Christ's complaint against them. He charged them with hypocrisy and said that the Pharisees were ethical slackers. "For I say unto you, That except your righteousness shall exceed the righteousness of the scribes and Pharisees, ye shall in no case enter into the kingdom of heaven" (Mt. 5:20). In the same way, we tend to think that a man who yells and blusters and intimidates has an excess of strength. We think he has a surplus. But biblically understood, he is actually a covenant wimp.

We should see that instructed by biblical wisdom, strength and tenderness are not actually two different things. We may picture the two together by means of various analogies in combination—velvet and brick—but the two things together actually constitute one virtue, a virtue we may identify as essential to biblical masculinity.

This is why he should understand the foundations of his strength and the necessary results of it, and then, with understanding, try a little tenderness.

CHAPTER 9

TWO BY SIX

N ormally I don't like wooden definitions, but the versatility of wood is such that there are some forms of definition that are done best with wood.

In building a house, the external walls are normally constructed from two-by-sixes spaced sixteen inches apart. On one of his rare visits to our building site, the building inspector tried to talk me into spacing the studs two feet apart, but I wanted structural stability more than I wanted the improvement in insulation efficiency. Regardless, the framed wall of wood defines the boundaries of the house.

Consequently, this wall defines, for as long as the house stands, the difference between *inside* and *outside*. This wall provides support for the trusses, which support the roof, and thereby maintain the difference between *wet* and *dry*. This wall, unlike all the other walls in the house, has two faces. On the external side, the sheathing is fastened, the housewrap attached, and then the siding. On the internal side of the same wall, the sheetrock is screwed on, just like all the other interior walls. Most interior walls are solid, but this perimeter wall, which defines the house, is filled with windows.

Good wood has cured somewhat, and when you cut the metal bands holding a lot together, the two by sixes don't suddenly curl up like they were specialty french fries or something. They will usually have a moderate crown which can be identified by looking down the length of the wood, and it is a good idea to have the crowns all on the same side of the wall.

These two by sixes are not finish wood—no one is going to try to make cupboards out of them—and the point is for most of their value to be completely out of sight. At the same time, they are usually fir, and freshly cut fir has a delightful smell.

Husbands are a lot like these two-by-sixes. They have a responsibility to define the boundaries of the family—what is the difference between inside and outside. The husband and father is called to name, and know by naming, the members of his family. When Scripture requires us to refrain from coveting anything that is our neighbor's, it is assuming this kind of wooden, and very rigid, definition.

Husbands and fathers are to support the roof. Their duty of protection and provision is fundamental. Because of the support of the roof, children are warm and dry instead of cold and wet. They should grow to maturity, and in this grow to the point where they no longer take all this for granted. But when they are little, it is the father's duty to see to it that they take it for granted. A man's wife doesn't take him for granted, but she trusts and believes him—and she was there at the wedding ceremony when he promised that he would support the roof.

A husband has two sides, just like the exterior wall. The side of the wall that faces his family is very much like the other walls of the house. The sheetrock is the same, the texturing is the same, the color of the paint is the same, pictures are hung, and so on. This means that the man of the house is to live with his family *as family*. The face he presents to them is conducive to the warmth of life together. But unlike the other walls, six inches away from the warmth of the living room is the hard snow or cold rain. And he has to deal with this at the same time. He presents a wall of protective siding to the world and warmth to his family.

Some men have trouble with performing these two tasks rightly. Some have the hard protective siding facing both ways, so that they are hard against the world and hard against their own family. Others—sensitive, modern males—have sheetrock on both sides, and the sheetrock doesn't weather well. A few men—the worst kind of all—have sheetrock against the elements and siding on the inside.

The perimeter wall has windows in it, and these are to enable those who live in the house the pleasure of seeing the world. A husband and father is to *teach*. He is to show his family what the outside is like. The family should be able to look through the worldview windows he supplies and come to see and understand what is happening outside. These windows enable the family to see, but they must perform the same protective functions that the wall does. And this calls for great wisdom—how to explain the world to the children without exposing them to it. Some men opt out and "protect" their children by leaving out the windows. Others let their kids deal with the world without protection and direction—these are not windows but simply holes in the wall.

A good man isn't warped. He has cured somewhat, he is mature. Many young men believe they are ready for a family because they have come from a tree that is the right size. Freshly milled at the age of nineteen, they believe they are prepared to be built into a wall right now because their dimensions are right. They are two-by-six and ten feet long, but when you cut the metal band, they still *sproing* all over the driveway.

It is important to remember that the two-by-six husband is not necessarily finish wood. It is far easier to get splinters from handling this wood than from the hard wood meant to build a coffee table. He is not the prettiest thing, especially with that Boise Cascade stamp on top of the knot. This is wood that is meant to be nailed, meant to be fixed, meant to be cut. And when a saw runs through this kind of wood, the smell—an aroma of sacrifice—is one of the sweetest smells on earth.

CHAPTER 10

WARRIOR WUSS

T he American military is currently acting the part of a weak sister. The pressure is on to bring women into combat roles. Our military is going along, in its inimitable and craven way, with this declared intention to feminize the armed forces. The military hierarchy is crushing any principled objections that might arise within the ranks. Of course, as the current drill requires, the Church stands mutely by, wondering what on earth this might all mean. Probably a sign of the end times. Indications of our cultural rot and dissolution are legion these days, but this one ranks in the top five.

Not surprisingly, the problem can be traced back to the condition of the Christian family. Men do not understand that when they take a wife, they are to determine their subsequent duties from a careful scrutiny of the Word of God. They are not to take their orders from the spirit of the secular age. Neither are they to catch the latest feel-good wave of revival excitement which is filling up our nation's stadiums with deep-throated panty-waists. About the only thing missing from the evangelical masculine renewal movement today would be the breast implants.

Understanding our enemy, and then fighting him, never occurs to us. Our culture can perpetrate the most monstrous outrages against nature, and we evangelicals scurry around the edges of the orgy, trying to give somebody a tract. "Too busy right now? Okay! Maybe later!" Brighten the corner where you are.

Not one denomination which supports chaplains in the military has taken a stand against women in combat. Not one Christian parachurch organization serving the military has taken a stand against women in combat. This is not the source of the problem—even these things are symptomatic. The broad failure of masculinity within our culture is a failure within the *home*, and, in particular, within *each* home.

Masculine duties are manifold, but surely one of the central duties of a husband is to protect his wife from harm. "Remember the Lord, great and awesome, and fight for your brethren, your sons, your daughters, your wives, and your houses" (Neh. 4:14b, NKJV). When necessary, he does this in concert with other men who are defending their families as well. This is the divine order established by God, and only impudence disputes it.

This does not mean that the guys should fight when they are drafted by the collectivist State to lower the price of oil a few pennies per gallon. Rather, it means that husbands should accept as part of their central masculine identity the role of lord protector. Not only must this role be accepted, it must be felt in the bones. Christian men still fight, and many of them fight courageously and well, but almost no Christian men understand what fighting is supposed to mean.

A nation defended by her women is a nation no longer worth defending. When women are placed in the front line of defense, every Christian man should walk away from the cause of that nation as being beneath contempt. Taking this a step further, a nation as far gone as to think that women in combat is a viable way to go is a nation which is no longer defensible in principle—even if there remains a misguided desire to defend it. Men who understand their duties in this regard, or men who are willing to *recover* an understanding of their duties, should recognize that the result of all our evangelical dithering is that the nation which we call the United States *has already been lost.*

This means that men should begin to think through their responsibilities regarding the next round. This statement is not made in a column on the civil magistrate, but rather as an exhortation to *husbands.* A man must protect his family, and in the coming years a thinking man will be looking for a good hill to defend. How might that be done? Families should begin congregating in communities where these duties are understood, and the men of those communities have every intention of fulfilling those duties.

Christian men who are in the military should get out at the first lawful opportunity, and move to a community where they may defend their families instead of their current unwilling defense of the feminist agenda—which agenda appears at present to be a desire to turn the U.S. Navy into an offshore brothel.

When God brings judgment upon a culture, that judgment is sometimes catastrophic. We sometimes debate among ourselves whether the coming judgment will be in that category or just a divine tap on the wrist. It does not occur to us to look at what has already happened. Neither does it occur to us to consider biblically the *magnitude* of what we have done.

The prohibition to women in Deuteronomy 22:5 is one which blindsides us. We knew abortion and homosexuality were abominations, but here we are told, no woman shall put on "the gear of a warrior" (*keli gabar*). But why not? "The woman shall not wear that which pertaineth unto a man, neither shall a man put on a woman's garment: *for all that do so are abomination* unto the LORD thy God" (Deut. 22:5).

We are far gone in our commitment to these follies. A commercial for the Armed Forces can come on the television, and there we see a sweet little feminine face peering out at us from the depths of her helmet, like a lonely pea in a soup bowl. And still we sit quietly, solemn as a judge.

CHAPTER 11

A HOME IN THE RIGHT KEY

W e often do not pay enough attention to what key we are in. We may pay close attention to what we are currently "playing" and what note comes next, but not enough concern is shown for the overall effect. What key are we in?

Another way of saying this is that we defend and explain ourselves in the details, not recognizing that we have created a context that in effect completely dominates those details. There are many examples of this—in theology, in politics, and in family life. Just one example from theology should suffice to illustrate the point. In Reformed theology, many have adopted a certain understanding of the "covenant of works" and the "covenant of grace." In this view, Adam was placed in the garden under a strictly legal covenant. He sinned against this covenant of works, and so then

God established a covenant of grace. The problem is that the covenant of strict justice has already established what key we are in, and it is next to impossible to keep the works from that first covenant from seeping in to corrupt the grace of the second.

It would be far better to see that God Himself is an eternally covenanted Godhead of persons. The Father does not love the Son in a covenant of works, but rather as a fountainhead of inexhaustible covenanted love. If we understand this as the "ultimate" covenant, then we will find that it is love and goodness and favor that keeps seeping into our lives. That is what we want; that is our sanctification. In other words, the key we establish at the beginning of our music is crucial.

So, how does this apply to marriage? In many ways, we see the same tangles we get into in our theology duplicating themselves in our relationships with our spouses. A man and his wife are bound together by covenant. This much is plain in Scripture (Mal. 2:14; Prov. 2:17). But is it a covenant of works or a covenant of grace? Paul commands husbands to love their wives as Christ loved the Church, and he commands wives to respect and honor their husbands in the same way that the Church does Christ. This means that the covenant we are to imitate is the new covenant, a covenant of grace.

But this means we must really understand *grace*. Not only must we understand grace, we must be able to see it as the ultimate reality in which we live and move and have our being. Because we are sinners, we can be surrounded by grace and still not be able to see it. Going back to the covenant with Adam in the garden, many theologians look at this and see a situation calling for raw obedience and strict, merited justice. But this misses the wonderful context. God created Adam, placed him in a luxurious garden, created a beautiful woman to be with him, and gave him all the fruit in the garden to eat with just one tree excepted. He even allowed him to eat from the tree of life. He walked with Adam in the garden in the cool of the day. This is all grace, unmerited favor. Adam had done nothing to deserve it. Like all grace, it created obligations, but there is a vast difference between a gracious obligation and a legal obligation.

When conflict arises in a marriage that has the keynote of works and not grace, somebody hauls out the contract. Imagine a husband, Bible open to Ephesians 5, his finger jabbing at the verse that says she should be submissive. "Why aren't *you* keeping your end of this deal?" Let us assume for a moment that he is right about the facts of the particular conflict, and let us assume that she should have been submissive and was not. Nevertheless, his behavior here shows that he is in the wrong key entirely. He wants the right thing done on the basis of a demand rather than wanting grace (*his* grace) to generate its own completely different kind of demand.

Things are complicated further by that perverse sinfulness that wants to hold our spouse to a covenant of works while insisting that they should see us in the light of a covenant of grace. In other words, "When I sin, what does she expect? I'm not Jesus. Doesn't she know how to forgive?" But when *she* sins, we can't believe it. "Look at this verse. What's her problem? Can't she read?" In other words, *my* sin is a human foible. *Her* sin is perverse obstinacy. It reminds me of the old self-serving conjugation of a certain irregular verb— "I am firm. You are stubborn. He is pig-headed."

The basic question here is whether law operates in the context of grace, or whether grace operates in the surrounding context of law. If the former, then marriage is delight upon delight. If the latter, then it is one conflict after another. In these two different marriages, the objective standards may be exactly the same, but they are played in different keys.

Now a marriage defined and shaped by grace is not an antinomian marriage. Grace has a backbone. Grace can be sinned against, and it can (and should) object when this happens. But everything depends on *how* this happens. Law within the defining context of grace is true law. Law outside that context always rots and spreads the contamination to everything it touches—including what many husbands expect from their wives.

CHAPTER 12

HOW TO EXASPERATE YOUR WIFE

Not that I am an expert or anything.

A woman comes into marriage with a certain set of naive assumptions about the density of her sweet baby's head. Some husbands may want their wives to develop a more realistic understanding, and that *ipso pronto*. If this is in fact the case, then certain trusty devices have been employed by more industrious husbands over the years, and they have worked in a very effective manner to this end.

The first and most important thing to do is take a very strong stand on male leadership. By strong stand, I mean as measured in decibels and not by performance. The disparity between the two may draw unfavorable attention and reviews, marring the surface of domestic tranquility from time to time. When this happens, a man should demand in a loud, blustering voice why it is necessary to speak in *that* tone of voice. It seemed disrespectful.

Another device, favored by men who do not want to come off as a more traditional male, is that of pseudo-sensitivity. Great concern must be expressed over the possible neglect of her vocational gifts and career opportunities. If this is played right, a woman can be maneuvered into working a full-time job alongside her husband's, and all without her being relieved of any of her full-time responsibilities in the home. The enterprising husband can find himself with one job and two incomes, and he then has the opportunity to figure out ways to spend the money while she is spending her evenings doing the laundry.

And a woman should not be allowed to spend very much money. In a strange kind of way, she might even learn to derive great satisfaction in how long she can make her fifty bucks last. In the meantime, her husband can spend money on a good bass boat, beer, a chop saw, a hunting rifle, beer, videos, that extra cable service carrying ESPN, and beer. When asked about this, he might intone that it would not be good to be penny-wise and pound-foolish. If she still asks for money to buy some clothes or shoes for herself, he should give her the money but act slightly disappointed in her desire to spend it on herself. He should not *say* anything, and if questioned about his silence, he should say, "No, that's all right. Hm."

A man should take special care to give his wife permission to home school. She has been asking for a couple years, and if he gives permission, this will keep her quiet for a couple more. Then, when she asks for some direction, discipline, or leadership in curriculum decisions, he can gently remind her that *she* was the one who requested that they do this.

Fussiness over meals is also important. It is not important *how* the fussiness is exhibited, but it is essential that it *be* exhibited. One man may want to demand his food at six o' clock, straight up, another may want his food piping hot, and yet another may want to insist on an entire absence of whatever vegetable it is that annoys him.

He should make sure he talks about how various women at work, or at church, are good-looking. Just as a general observation, nothing important. Nevertheless, it is encouraging to note that more and more women are keeping themselves up these days. On a related note, he should be concerned about his wife's weight, and he should vocalize his concern from time to time in a helpful tone of voice. Unless he tells her that she has inadvertently put on a few pounds, she would probably never know.

He must require at all times that she is never allowed to know more than he does in any area. If by happenstance she does, then there should be an unspoken assumption in the household that she should keep quiet about it. To do otherwise would be disrespectful.

He must ensure that the television is on from the time he gets home until about ten-thirty or eleven. It will provide a comforting backdrop to the conversation and life of the family. If the television is on all the time, it provides a certain wallpaper for the mind, filling in those awkward si-lences. The wife should be given every opportunity of learn-ing what shows and sporting events are important to him.

And of course, at the end of the day, when the lights are turned down low, he should head off to bed like a sim-ple-minded juggins, acting the part of a grinning prospector who is expecting to find a sexual El Dorado any minute now. And let's all wish him some luck.

THE MEANING
OF SEX

CHAPTER 13

OF HIS FLESH AND OF HIS BONES

usbands are summoned by Scripture to love their wives in a particular way, loving their wives as they understand the love of Christ for His bride, the Church. They are to do this because the words of Genesis apply to Christ and the Church on one level, and they apply to each marriage on another. And each marriage, in its turn, speaks of Christ and the Church. This is a deep mystery, Paul says, but there it is.

> So ought men to love their wives as their own bodies. He that loveth his wife loveth himself. For no man ever yet hated his own flesh; but nourisheth and cherisheth it, even as the Lord the church: For we are members of his body, of his flesh, and of his bones. For this cause shall a man leave his father and mother, and shall be joined unto his wife, and they two shall be one flesh. This is a great mystery: but I speak concerning Christ and the church (Eph.5:28–32).

His words weave in and out, and it is impossible for us to grasp all that is here. It is hard to say if Paul even grasped it—he is the one who confessed it a great mystery, even though he was the one writing under the inspiration of the Holy Spirit.

Consider how it weaves in a paraphrase. Men ought to love their wives as they already do love their own physical bodies. The man who loves his wife is actually loving himself in another form or manifestation, and this returns to him in a blessing. No one ever mistreats his own physical body—rather, he feeds it and keeps it warm. This is just how the Lord treats the church. He does this because we are His body, of His flesh and of His bones, as Genesis said of the first man and woman. A man shall leave his father and mother and be joined to his wife sexually, and as a result the two are one flesh. She is bone of his bone and flesh of his flesh, and therefore it is appropriate for a man to marry a woman. Because Eve was bone of Adam's bone and flesh of Adam's flesh, it was fitting for them to be joined together as one flesh in sexual union. Moreover, it has been fitting (ever since) for any given man to leave his father and mother and be joined to his wife and to become one flesh with her.

Christ took on bone of our bone, and flesh of our flesh in the Incarnation. As a result of this, it is fitting for Him to be joined together with His bride, the Church. Because of the Incarnation in the past, we may look forward to the Consummation of all things in the future. Because we share one flesh with Christ, we may become one flesh with Christ.

This is what Christian husbands are told to imitate. "Husbands, love your wives, *even as* Christ also loved the church, and gave himself for it" (Eph. 5:25). As Paul said elsewhere in another context, who is sufficient for these things? The answer is obvious that no one is sufficient for them at all, and yet the command remains. As married men, we are required to note two aspects of ourselves—*"myself in myself"* and *"myself in another."* We do this not to separate them but rather just the reverse.

In the grip of modern individualism, we see two people, and that is all. The Bible requires us to see a fundamental unity here. Theologians speak of *totus Christus* to refer to the "whole Christ," a Christ that includes His bride, the Church. We *are* the body of Christ, the Bible tells us repeatedly. In an analagous way, a woman is the body of her husband. The two of them together are *one*, the whole man.

What difference does this make? Paul concludes this section by saying that every man, in particular, should love his wife *even as himself* (v. 33). In one sense, this is nothing other than an application of the second greatest commandment. We are required to love our neighbors as ourselves, and Jesus told a story that made it abundantly clear that our neighbor is to be defined as pretty much anybody in the world. But in another sense, this teaching in Ephesians 5 transcends that general commandment. I am told to love my neighbor *as if* he were myself. I am told to love my wife because she *is* myself. My neighbor is one flesh with me in the sense that we are both descended from Adam. A wife is one flesh with her husband in the sense that the two of them, both descended from Adam, have come together sexually. They have completed the circle.

The second "one flesh" is made possible by the first. God's pattern of death and resurrection is seen in how He established marriage. Adam was put into a deep sleep, a clear type of death, and his wife was taken from his side. Because God made the one into two, Adam named her *Ishshah*, bone of his bones and flesh of his flesh. Because God had made the one into two, it was possible for the two to become one.

Put another way, God broke Adam and the two pieces were a man and a woman. These two pieces were fashioned in such a way as to enable them to come back together again, and the round trip meant that the man was much more complete. A solitary one became two so that two could become a unified one.

Does anyone get this? I don't think so. In the meantime, husbands should meditate on it and treat their wives far better than they do.

CHAPTER 14

SEXUAL GLORY

B efore addressing our subject directly, we must begin with a number of apparently disconnected data.
Throughout his book, the prophet Isaiah described
the days of messianic glory in many magnificent ways. In
one place, he says, "And the Lord will create upon every
dwelling place of mount Zion, and upon her assemblies,
a cloud and smoke by day, and the shining of a flaming
fire by night: for upon all the glory shall be a defence" (Is.
4:5). In the NKJV, "defence" is rendered as "covering."
John Newton rendered this passage wonderfully in his
hymn "Glorious Things of Thee Are Spoken."

> Round each habitation hov'ring,
> See the cloud and fire appear
> For a glory and a cov'ring,
> Showing that the Lord is near!

"For a glory and a covering"—the Shekinah glory that accompanied Israel was a beautiful shelter, a magnificent fortress, a glory and a covering. Given this wonderful image, the apostle Paul makes a profound application.

> For a man indeed ought not to cover his head, forasmuch as he is the image and glory of God: but the woman is the glory of the man. . . . For this cause ought the woman to have power on her head because of the angels. . . . Doth not even nature itself teach you, that, if a man have long hair, it is a shame unto him? But if a woman have long hair, it is a glory to her: for her hair is given her for a covering (1 Cor. 11:7, 10, 14–15).

As we see, the words *glory* and *covering* go very well together indeed. Given the background in Isaiah, this cannot be a coincidence.

Paul teaches that a woman should cover her head with long hair precisely because she is the glory of her husband. Her hair is *her* glory, and in turn she is *his* glory. Thus, her hair, when a covering, is the glory of her husband. This glory is manifested to all, in the presence of angels. Further, her long hair is placed upon her head not just to show that she is under authority, but also to show that she *wields* it. Several chapters earlier, Paul has reminded married couples that a wife exercises sexual authority over her husband (1 Cor. 7:4). And the nature of this submission and authority is displayed to the world in a wife's hair.

But we are sophisticated moderns, and this is all too weird. Most Christians today dismiss this passage as "just a cultural thing." And those few Christians who *do* believe that the passage is binding today think that it is talking about women of severe countenance dressed in gray with a doily on top of their heads. No one thinks of it in terms of a biblical eroticism.

We can first dismiss the idea that this passage simply reflects first-century mores and customs and nothing more. Paul says that these truths are taught by nature itself, which is quite a different thing than being required by Graeco-Roman customs. The appeal to nature is an appeal to the *creation* order and not an appeal to time-bound customs. Paul clearly intends this teaching to be normative in the church throughout all generations. He teaches us that this is the way things *are* in the very nature of the world and we must learn to conform to it. And if hair is a woman's glory, the question before us should surely not be how short it can be before it *stops* being a glory. There is a good answer to this question, but why are we asking it?

Of course, those who "obey" the passage with all appropriate reactionary prune-like glumness are missing the point equally. We are talking about declaring glory and not about being dour.

The marriage relationship is a private sexual relationship, but one publicly recognized and honored (Heb. 13:4). Those things which are public emblems of this relationship should reflect the nature of it accurately, but this is particularly the case with emblems which are given to us in Scripture. Rings are nice (and lawful), but God has assigned another way of making the declaration.

A woman's hair is designed by God to make a statement to the world. When she wears her hair the way she should, it demonstrates her submission and her authority, it shows her gentleness and her power. A godly woman is sweet, gentle, submissive, and terrible as an army with banners. Her glory shows that she is her husband's sexual covering, a formidable defense and wall of protection for him.

Husbands, what is your wife to you? If you have a decent marriage, you could probably answer in greeting card terms: "She is my best friend," or "She is a wonderful mother to my children." But if you have a biblical marriage, the answer should be quite different: "She is my *glory*."

CHAPTER 15

SEXUAL GRUMBLING

A good marriage is characterized by an ability to talk about anything. This does not mean that it is easy to talk about everything, but rather that any subject can be addressed in a way that is profitable.

One area where talking can be difficult is in the area of sex—particularly in discussing the sexual temptations which come at the relationship from outside. Because sexual discussion between husband and wife can be difficult for many reasons, there are a number of things that a husband should remember as he takes responsibility for undertaking such risky business. At the center of everything is his duty of Christian contentment.

First, a husband should be clear in his mind that he is talking about his temptations and not giving way to them. In short, talking should be honest talking and not a form of discontented manipulation. He should understand what his temptations actually are and what they are not. His wife should be able to help him *resist* those things which are temptations to sin. If he doesn't believe something is sin, but talks to her as though he is "struggling" with it, he is actually trying to manipulate or corrupt her, not talk with her. More than one man has "confessed" certain things to his wife when he was actually trying to corrupt her with them.

Another issue is that honor and praise always edify every aspect of a relationship, including sex, while grumbling is destructive and tears down. Many men are chronic sexual complainers, and Scripture forbids complaining (Phil. 2:14) and requires contentment (Phil. 4:11). Further, the Bible says that men are to honor their wives (1 Pet. 3:7), and this includes expressing honor to them for their sexual attractiveness. Godly contentment is *closely* related to an undefiled marriage bed (Heb. 13:4–5). Put another way, many men think they are tempted by lust when they are *really* tempted more by a discontented and critical spirit.

In many cases, they wouldn't dream of complaining about their food life the way they complain about their sex life. But complaining always tears down. A man who complained about the food all the time is unlikely to see an improvement in the cooking. It is the same in the bedroom—a man who complains about sex all the time is unlikely to see improvement in the cooking there either. This remains true *even if all his complaints remain unspoken.* Complaining is communicated in countless ways.

Complaints can be divided into three categories. The first is that a man's wife does not look like other women. We may call this the adulterous complaint. A man is told to be satisfied with his wife's breasts (Prov. 5:19), and this excludes the common practice that many men have of getting their appetite abroad while eating at home. An undiscriminating man who has a steady diet of movies and television shows he shouldn't be watching is going to grow increasingly discontented with his wife's appearance.

He might respond that he would be happy to be satisfied with his wife's breasts but that she won't let him near them, which leads to the second kind of complaint—not the way she looks to him, but the way she responds to him. Because her behavior is under her control, men sometimes assume that they have a right to complain here if they do not appreciate something. What these men do not realize is that a woman's sexual responsiveness flourishes, as a luxuriant green plant in the garden, in direct correlation to how it is nourished and watered. Many men complain that their wives are too embarrassed to be responsive and hot like the Shulamite, but *they* are too embarrassed to praise their own wives as that ancient husband did. And so we may call this the complaint of the fool.

The third complaint occurs when a wife is actively sinning against her husband, either through infidelity, gross lack of submission, refusal to have relations with him, and so on. If a woman is sinning in this way, a husband does not have the right to overlook the problem. If he cannot bring the situation around, then he is responsible to get help from the outside. If he refuses, but still complains, it is the complaint of a coward.

If a man knows that his desire to talk with his wife does not proceed from discontent, then a talk about all these things can be quite helpful. He should remember that a husband is responsible to help his wife not respond to him badly as he tries to talk with her. Many women have gotten themselves into a trap—they are offended when their husbands keep things back from them, but then they are offended in a different way if their husbands tell them any details about their temptations. In short, they penalize honesty and penalize dishonesty. When wives do this, a man can't win for losing, and so he frequently winds up clever and dishonest when he needs to become wise and honest. It is all well and good to say that a woman shouldn't respond this way, but the husband is the one responsible to help her work through this. She is given to him as a helper, and one of the things he needs help with is sexual fidelity (1 Cor. 7:2). And marriage is a help with this in other ways than simply providing physical sexual release. Godly conversation is an important part of it.

But in order to provide true help, the foundation of all discussion between a Christian husband and wife must be contentment. A contented man and woman can strive to glorify God still more in what they learn sexually. But if the striving is built on *discontent*, then everything they learn how to do will only serve to exacerbate that discontent.

CHAPTER 16

SEVEN EFFECTIVE STRATEGIES FOR DEALING WITH LUST

1. Run away. Paul tells Timothy to "flee youthful lusts" (2 Tim. 2:22). Joseph employed this admirable technique when dealing with Potiphar's wife (Gen. 39:12), and he did not know that in running from her arms, he was actually running toward a throne. This was not made immediately obvious to him, but it was a key element in that story. Would you excel in your work? Would you stand before kings? Would you be entrusted with great things? Then run away from every breach of sexual trust. You are running *toward* a high calling.

2. Don't run away. There is a kind of fastidious "denial" of lust that just pours gasoline on the fire (Rom. 7:7). Putting a pressure cooker lid on and cinching it down tight—while

keeping the heat on—is a good way to get beans on the ceiling. See the next chapter, "Nuisance Lust."

3. Don't get everything backwards. Remember that there will be a natural tendency to apply Rule #1 when you should apply Rule #2, and #2 when you should apply #1. Study your lusts. Undertake this study with the full knowledge that your lusts are liars, and so is the devil. Look *at* your lusts instead of looking *with* them. When you look with your lusts, you will see many curvaceous delights. When you look at your lusts, all you can see is a little chimp with bright red lipstick on. Find out what's actually going on. This is no contradiction.

Should we answer a fool according to his folly, or not? It depends on the circumstance (Prov. 26:4-5). If you learn how to study your lusts, you will soon discover that porn is a bundle of catechetical lies. Study your lusts (and not the object of your lust), and you will come to see the lying trick that makes porn attractive.

When it comes to studying your lusts as an adversary, John Owen had something quite helpful to say.

"This is the way men deal with their enemies. They search out their plans, ponder their goals, and consider how and by what means they have prevailed in the past. Then, they can be defeated. This is a most important strategy. If you do not utilize this great strategy, your warfare is very primitive. We need to know how sin uses occasions, opportunities, and temptations to gain advantage. Search its pleas, pretences, reasonings, strategies, colours, and excuses. We need to trace this serpent in all of its windings, and to recognize its most secret tricks: 'This is your usual way, and course; I know what you aim at" . . . bring it to the law of God and love of Christ" (John Owen, *Voices From the Past*, p. 56).

4. Make careful distinctions. Distinguish between mere physical appetite, which is certainly part of this equation, and lust, which is the foundational culprit. There is no such thing as a biological need to break God's law, and your "members which are on the earth" want to break God's law (Col. 3:5). That's the whole point. That's what makes it attractive in the first place. Biological appetite must be directed and disciplined (1 Thess. 4:4), while lust must be killed (Rom. 8:13). Don't capture your chief lust, and then act like Ahab did, inviting Benhadad up into his chariot (1 Kings 20:33-34). This is a basic lesson of sexual ethics—never invite defeated lusts up into your chariot.

5. Recognize that lust is wired up to quite a few other attitudes of yours that you probably don't think of as sexual at all. But lust is not just a straight line desire (as the physical appetite is), but is rather part of a complex web of tangled relationships, competitions, envies, resentments, discontents, strivings, comparings, and sidelong glancings. This complex web involves *lots* of other people—your father, your mother, your brothers, your sisters, your friends, your foes—all of them connected in some mysterious way to that unruly creature in your loins. Fights come from lusts (Jas. 4:1), and lusts come from fights. Driven by lust, masturbation is not a solo act. Everybody is involved—some as

victims, others as co-perpetrators, and some as both. Lust is therefore inescapably social.

6. Virtues and vices are like grapes—they come in bunches. Lusts are connected to everything else, but so is self-control. The fruit (singular) of the Spirit is nine-fold—love, joy, peace, patience, kindness, gentleness, goodness, faithfulness, and self-control (Gal. 5:22). Just as lust goes with envy, strife, discontent, and so on; so self-control goes with patience, kindness, and joy. Godly discipline is not hermetically sealed into one little compartment of your life. It affects everything, and spreads to everything. Godly discipline expands and grows. When you get up early to study, when you take on the kind of job that creates calluses, when you run three miles daily, you are becoming a certain kind of person. You cannot say that you would rather sit on a couch all day in order to fully concentrate on your sexual purity.

7. Recognize that sexual sin is not just a sin for which there will be consequences later (although that is true)—sexual sin is itself a judgment for antecedent sin. Find out what that sin is, and deal with it. Stop floating down toward the falls. Work your way upstream. "The mouth of strange women is a deep pit: he that is abhorred of the LORD shall fall therein" (Prov. 22:14). Analogously, homosexual sin is not just a sin with consequences, it is itself a consequence of another sin (Rom. 1:18, 24). So sexual sin isn't just the bait that makes another trap work—something else was the bait for which *this* is the trap. "For a whore is a deep ditch; and a strange woman is a narrow pit. She also lieth in wait as for a prey, and

increaseth the transgressors among men" (Prov. 23:27-28). If you were to fall into this deep ditch, it would be a profound blow from God.

So not all sexual covetousness is lust. When a man gives way to lust *simpliciter* the end result is arousal. When a man gives way to sexual covetousness, the end result is discontent and a vague sense of entitlement.

Here is the distinction. In Romans 7, the apostle Paul says that he would not have known what sin was if the law had not said "do not covet" (Rom. 7:7). The rich young ruler comes to Jesus, and claims to have kept the entire second table of the law, with the one exception that Jesus left out of His list—the prohibition of covetousness (Mark 10:19). We have to remember that one of the prohibited objects of covetousness was found in the person of your neighbor's *wife* (Ex. 20:17).

In Proverbs 5, a young man is instructed, bottom line, to stay out of the wrong beds. He is told to avoid adultery (Prov. 5:20), and he is told this because the Lord is omniscient and sees everything that is going on (Prov. 5:21). The relevance to my point here is found in the preceding verses, where the husband is told to rejoice with the wife of his youth (Prov. 5:18). He is told to let her breasts satisfy him at all times, and to be ravished, enraptured, delighted, and intoxicated with her love (Prov. 5:19). That's hard to do when you have been out window shopping for other models. Or supermodels.

The progression toward adultery moves like this—simmering discontent, open discontent, open desire in other directions, which is lust, and then the lust acted out, with infidelity as the result. Now a man might be able to convince himself that he is not being unfaithful in the first two stages—he is not being aroused, and he is not actively seeking that kind of gratification. His problem doesn't appear to him to be overtly sexual at all. But that's a set up. Don't feed the kind of discontent that will, later on, feed something else.

CHAPTER 17

NUISANCE LUST

Note: This is a letter to an imaginary husband. The situation of this couple is assembled as a composite from various counseling situations.

Dear Tony,

Thanks for the email and the follow-up phone call. I am glad you decided to get help with this, and I am glad that you and Suzanne are talking about it. A central part of this letter will be some advice on how to make those talks more profitable.

Let me summarize the problem as you outlined it, so that we can be sure I've got it right. Your marriage is solid, you think the world of Suzanne, and she of you, your sex life is robust, and you love your family. Your wife does not doubt your Christian commitments at all. At the same time, from time to time you are distracted by various lusts—not the triple x stuff, nothing hard core or marriage threatening—but

73

enough to hurt your wife significantly whenever you stumble or you try to talk with her about it. Whenever you talk about it (because you are confessing having fallen into some sin), you are in the doghouse and the talks are not productive. Whenever you are trying to anticipate a problem, she doesn't understand what you are talking about at all, and cannot comprehend why you would be bringing it up. Does this sum up the situation reasonably well? If it does, it may help you in knowing you are not the lone weirdo. A lot of Christian husbands are in this situation.

Now, what I am going to explain to you does not fall under the heading of "lighten up, it's not that bad." Rather, it is "lighten up or it is going to *get* really bad." What you are dealing with could be called nuisance lust. At the same time, unaddressed, porn can be a marriage destroyer, and nothing I am going to say here should be taken as minimizing the impact of infidelity in marriage, whether actual infidelity or computer-induced fantasy infidelity. The thing to learn is how to turn away from unedifying stuff in a way that does not churn up nuisance lusts inside, in a way that makes things worse. Christian husbands have to learn how to stop trying to put out these fires with buckets of gasoline.

There is a form of lust that is more a function of your relationship to the "protective" laws you have created than it is a about your relationship to another woman's body. It even works this way with God's law (Rom. 3:20; 5:20).

But with God's law, you are not allowed to give yourself a pass as a way of getting around this problem. The way to deal with the law that God laid down is by turning to Christ—that is one of the ways the law was designed to work. But the same principle we learn about God's law and our justification also applies to our own laws, and our sanctification. We must learn to use laws as a reason to turn to Christ for grace and wisdom *and not as a source of spiritual power in themselves.*

I am talking here about the fences around the law that we tend to build for ourselves, thinking that *rules* can fix these things. Well, they don't. Your laws can't bring the power for godliness in sanctification any more than God's law can bring justification. The divine law is a schoolmaster that makes us aware of our need for grace. Your house laws for your use of the family computer don't have any more sanctifying power than God's law does, right? How could they?

Paul would not have known the wretchedness of his sin if the law had not said, "Do not covet." Remember that the centerpiece of that commandment was the reminder not to covet your neighbor's *wife* (Ex. 20:17). Your lusts are the hornet's nest, and God's law is the stick that whacks it. This is done so that we will turn to Christ, but for some reason we think that after we have turned to Christ, we can grow in sanctification by whittling some extra sticks of our own for whacking the remainders of that hornet's nest. But whacking that nest always gets the same results, whether the rules are God's or yours. And it gets the same results even if your rules are good and wise—*especially* if they are good and wise.

Now there is obviously a delicate balance here, because the point is not to drop the rules so that you can go watch images that are corrosive to your soul. The point is not to grant yourself a looser set of permissions so that you can entertain yourself with porn lite. This is not "go ahead and sin" counsel. The point is to grant yourself a looser set of permissions *so that* you can walk away from it, for the right reasons, without leaving your heart back in front of the computer keyboard, wishing the better part of you hadn't turned the dern thing off.

There are two steps in this process. The first is that you have to get your mind around what I am explaining. You can't just check the right box. You have to *get* it. Second, after you get it, you need to show this letter to Suzanne, and work through it with her. Her first reaction will probably be something like, "Do you *agree* with this?" Or perhaps she will phrase it differently. "You don't agree with this, do you?" If you have internalized it rightly, the answer will be *yes*, but you should then be able to talk about it in a way that won't be offensive to her, or a stumbling block for her. Hope this makes sense.

So let me explain. Suppose you are sitting at your computer, and some blonde bikini-clad welterweight pops up on the screen. Imagine three possible responses from you, with your wife observing those responses without your knowledge. The first response is when you give way to sin *simpliciter*. You lust after that babe, and worse, for a hour or so. Your wife would be upset with you, and rightly so. You would be in the doghouse, right where you belong. Sin is sin. Jesus said not to do that (Matt. 5:28), and you did it anyway. Solomon said that you should be satisfied with your wife's breasts (Prov. 5:19), and you weren't.

The second response would please your wife very much. You react like someone dumped a pan of scalding water in your lap. You yell, jump up, and turn off the computer, praying imprecatory psalms down upon the hairy heads of the manufacturers of red bikinis. Your wife admires your fortitude and godliness, and she is astonished at the holy alacrity with which you leapt toward the ceiling.

The third response is that you look at it for a few seconds, say "huh, I wonder where *her* mother got to," and then you head on over to Drudge to find out what Nancy Pelosi is doing.

Now in the first instance, your wife won't want to hear any explanations, which is good, because there aren't any good ones. In the second, she thinks explanations are not necessary, which is false. You have drawn the line in such a way as to look like Joe Godly to her, but the images you saw are eating at your innards even while we speak. This is because you are trying to get sanctified through an external application of the rules or the standards. In the third setting, you treated it with the seriousness it deserved, which is to say, not very much, but your wife might still be miffed—because you didn't bolt away in a nanosecond. Was he really casual about it, she wonders, or was he "dallying"?

But *actual* dallying more often occurs with the second scenario, not the third. She is getting her security from the rule, and you are trying to get security from the same place.

But you should know, in your heart, the true nature of the insecurity that is being generated. You sometimes feel like you have an impossible situation in your heart—whether or not you look at anything—and every time you try to explain it to her you have a tangled and unhappy conversation.

Here is another scenario. Suppose a man and his wife are out walking at the mall, and some chick is walking toward them, bouncing away like there's no tomorrow. If the couple walk past her, and he says "that's just terrible; I can't believe some people," and his wife agrees, and they walk to the other end of the mall, clucking their tongues, I would be willing to bet ten dollars that the spectacle was far more of a problem to him than he is letting on. But if he could say to his wife, "Is this a great country, or what?" the chances are much better that he is handling it right. The problem is this: if he says that to his wife, then *she* might have trouble handling it right. What does he *mean* by saying, "is this a great country or what?" It is *that* kind of thing, she fulminates, that is causing the country to descend into a sinkhole of corruption. And yeah, she's right about that. But we want to be the kind of men who can learn to see this sin rightly, including these delights of sexual lust being advertised by herpes on heels.

Now if the wife comes to her husband afterwards and says, "Was that girl at the mall a problem to you?" his answer should be, "That's the kind of thing that would be a problem if we couldn't talk and joke about it." If she takes offense immediately, then that is going to cause him to clam up, not wanting unnecessary conflict with a wife who is dear to him. And when he clams up, he is left alone with things in his head that he ought not to be left alone with. When that happens, petty sins grow into more significant sins.

Most Christian women think that lust happens to guys when they are in the presence of any image of a scantily clad whoosit, and they think that this lust just happens the way a bowling ball falls when you drop it. But this is not true. Far more is involved than simple stimulus and response. There is stimulus, response, law, grace, marriage, communion, context, and wisdom. If you shut it up inside your head, then it will be largely confined to stimulus and response, which is why you have such a struggle with it.

Now what Jesus prohibited was the lust. He didn't require that you drive that stretch of the freeway, that place where the skanky billboard is, with your eyes closed. He prohibited the wanting and desiring; He did not prohibit the seeing.

But yes, someone will say: The seeing leads inexorably to lusting, just like when you drop that bowling ball. Sure, it often does. That does happen. But my point here is that lurching away with the wrong understanding of your house rules *leads to lust more often*. The fact that your wife really likes those rules does not give those rules the power to protect her, even though she thinks they do. Let us say another pop-up twinkie appears on your computer, this time with a green bikini, and even less of it than the girl with the red one had. If you yell, and cry out, "Ackk! my eyes, my eyes!" then you are in far greater danger than if you say, "Well, huh. We are a mammalian species it seems. Go put some clothes on now, dearie. There's a good girl."

You see the strategy. Minimize the seriousness of this, but not so that you can feel good about indulging yourself. Minimize the seriousness of it so that you can walk away from a couple of big boobs without feeling like you have just fought a cosmic battle with principalities and powers in the heavenly places, for crying out loud. Or, if you like, in another strategy of seeing things rightly, you could nickname these breasts of other woman *as* the "principalities and powers." Whatever you do, take this part of life in stride like a grown-up. Stop reacting like a horny and conflicted twelve-year-old boy.

The problem you are fighting has far more to do with how you and your wife are thinking about this than it has to do with "that lingeried hazard over there." This is a *trick*, I am telling you. The snare is inside you. The more you lay extra layers of rules on top of those flickering images, the more they shine through. The more you can see them, the more you want to see. It is not like the rules work the same way layers of wool blankets might. The point is for you to be free of this stuff, and not to try to obey an arbitrary restriction. I am saying that the arbitrary restrictions are often counterproductive. *They don't work.* You doubt what I say? Look at your own experience. This is like the old joke where guy flexes his arm back and forth, and says, "Doctor, it hurts when I do this." The doctor said, "Well, don't do that." Whatever it is you are doing right now doesn't work, right? So try something that will. Quit hitting the tar baby.

Walk away because you want to, and you know that you really want to because you could stay if you wanted. You could not stay "if you wanted to" in order to give way to lust because God's Word speaks directly to that. But you could see it if you wanted, free of lust, and since that is lawful (but not necessary), you might as well leave. Leaving is the point, but you want it to be the right kind of leaving, because *otherwise you are not really leaving.*

John Owen once said that a man should not think he makes any progress in godliness who walks not daily over the bellies of his lusts. I am not arguing against this; I am arguing *for* it. What I am trying to communicate to you is that a vampire needs to have a stake driven through the heart. Stop pelting him with your homemade nerf balls.

I assume that you or Suzanne may have questions, and I am happy to try to answer them if I can.

Cordially in Christ,

Douglas Wilson

CHAPTER 18

SEX IN HEAVEN?

N ow that some men have begun to read this chapter simply because of the title, we may save them some time by answering the question immediately—no.

At the same time, the question remains an important one. There is a natural tendency among some Christians to give the right answer here for all the wrong reasons. More than a few Christians throughout the history of the church have had difficulty with the fact of sex *here*, and this is the basis for them thinking of sexual relations in heaven as a theological impossibility. But this is a rationalistic inheritance from the Greeks, and not the teaching of Scripture at all.

This means that in answering the question in the negative we have to do so in a way that does justice to the fundamental goodness of the created order, to the materiality of the resurrected body, and to the meaning of the metaphor provided by sexual relations.

Discussions of this question turn naturally to the exchange Christ had with the Sadducees. They brought up the woman with seven husbands, and if marital sexuality is a feature of resurrection life, then the Sadducean question holds. Whose wife is she? Far from exalting marriage, anyone who holds to marriage and sex (as we understand it) in the afterlife is actually advocating everlasting polygamy or polyandry. The resurrection does not involve us in such tangles.

Neither does it require that a husband and wife, dearest of friends here, will drift apart to mere acquaintance. When they have been there ten thousand years, bright shining as the sun, he will not run into her some aeon or other and say, "Oh, hi. It's you." Our form of marriage is not a heavenly institution, but neither is our form of divorce.

Throughout the creation week, God repeated His claim that the created order was good. After He created a solitary male, He said that it was *not* good. He then created Eve from Adam's side, and the creation of *man* was complete—male and female created He them. The world and all it contains, sexuality included, is blessed by God.

The coming resurrection is not a vaporization into spiritual ether. We are not Hellenists and do not hold to the immortality of a disembodied soul. We are Christians, and we believe in the resurrection of the body. In this resurrection, men will be resurrected *men* and women will be resurrected *women*.

When the apostle Paul addresses this question (and he does, actually, in several places), he argues that sexual union here is a dim shadow of an ultimate union. This is a great mystery, he says, but the point is Christ and the church. The man joined to a woman becomes one with her in flesh. But the one joined to the Lord Jesus becomes one with Him in spirit (1 Cor. 6:17). The former is a metaphor for a heavenly reality beyond our comprehension. But we have to take care here, because we have learned to understand the word *spirit* here as necessarily ethereal. Spiritual union does not mean ghostly union.

The Lord Jesus did not become a neutered or androgynous thing in the resurrection. He remained a man, but what this actually means transcends our understanding. He is the ultimate man, the glorious bridegroom. He purchased a bride for Himself, and the union between the last Adam and the last Eve is an everlasting one.

But for some this still disappoints—not because it is not glorious—but because we have not yet answered the question that every happily married couple still has. "What will my relationship to my wife or husband be like? I know that, as part of the Bride, we all will be united to Christ, but what of my union with *this* woman? *This* man?" The answer is that it does not yet appear what we shall be like, but our unbelief is revealed in our fear that whatever it is, it will involve a significant downgrade. We imagine that the only options are the same as what we have here, or a blundering or malicious eradication of every trace of what we have here. This reveals that we do not understand the fundamental *direction* of resurrection. We err because we do not know the Scriptures, or the power, goodness, and kindness of God.

When we learn that we will not be married in our mundane sense, we imagine that we will be *unmarried* in the mundane sense—and heaven is viewed as one great, big college and career church group. But in the resurrection, we will be meta-sexual beings. Whatever our relationships will be, it will be better than what we have now, very different from what we have now, and have a basic continuity with what we have now. But when we imagine "different," we want to imagine something ethereal, wispy, "spiritual." In contrast, life in the resurrection will be more real, more substantive, more material.

We may find an illustration for this in the subject of food. Paul himself uses food to illustrate a point about sex. Food for the stomach, and the stomach for food, Paul says, but God will destroy them both (1 Cor. 6:13). And at this mention of destruction, many gnostics cry, "Ha! Good riddance. See? It says *destroy.*" But this overlooks what God always does when He destroys. He raises to life again, and this is the whole point. The resurrection body always has an element of continuity to that which died, but it is also taken up qualitatively to a much higher degree of glory. The discontinuity is also great. What was dishonorable is now honorable. What was corruptible is now incorruptible. What was contemptible is now glorious.

So will there be food in heaven? Yes, of course—we will sit down at the wedding supper of the Lamb, and the feasting will be beyond all reckoning. And so will be the occasion for the feasting. Will there be food in heaven? Of course not.

CHAPTER 19

MORE ON SEX IN HEAVEN

I n his short book *The Great Divorce*, C.S. Lewis gives us a wonderful picture of the ultimate sexual sanctification in the resurrection. One of the ghosts visiting heaven in that story has a little red lizard on his shoulder that represents lust. After some conversation, an angel receives permission from the ghost to kill the lizard. When he has done so, the ghost is turned into one of the solid people of heaven, and the lizard, mangled and broken on the ground, comes back to life as a glorious stallion. The man, now redeemed, mounts the stallion, and they both ride off into the mountains, further up and further in. The lesson is clear—"nothing, not even the best and noblest, can go on as it now is. Nothing, not even what is lowest and most bestial, will not be raised again if it submits to death."

As I have mentioned before, the great danger in denying that there is sex in heaven (as we know it) is that we invariably interpret this as a downgrade. This is unbelief and it moves us entirely in the wrong direction. At the same time, if the marital relation continues in some fashion in heaven, and if this includes sexuality in some fashion, then a number of things follow. The Saducean question confronts us directly—and this means that either *sex* has to be completely transformed, or *marriage* has to be.

The gnostic solution is always to etherize the resurrection, making it ghostly. This gets rid of the Sadducean taunt, but at far too high a cost. We lose the materiality of the created order, which the Scriptures require us to see as established forever. Jesus rummaged in the fridge after His resurrection and ate some honeycomb and broiled fish (Luke 24:41–43), and Jesus Christ is the same yesterday, today, and forever (Heb. 13:8). Ghosts don't eat honeycomb, and so this sheds light on Paul's comment that both food and stomach will be destroyed (1 Cor. 6:13). Destroyed, yes, but how and in what direction? We tend to interpret "destruction" as annihilation rather than death followed by glorious resurrection.

Christ passed through the wall into the upper room, and yet He was able to eat while there. This is a problem for us because it never occurs to us that He passed through the wall because the *wall* was ghostly, and not because Christ's resurrection body was. Then we wonder how a ghost could eat fish, but the real problem is how that ghostly fish could have satisfied a true man.

In trying to puzzle this out, we can go three basic directions from our current material bodies. The first direction is *down*, and this gnostic alternative has already been roundly rejected. And good riddance. Whatever happens in the resurrection, we are not neutered or vaporized.

The second direction is transformation *out*, where the differences between heaven and earth are to be seen in terms of ethical newness. In other words, marriage is not what marriage is here (although sex still is). Consequently, polygamy is not polygamy, fornication is not fornication, virginity is not virginity. In other words, the material conditions of life (although glorious and incorruptible) remain largely what they are here, but the *meaning* of them is altered. If this is the case, the Sadducees were asking the wrong question—trying to fit square, non-resurrection pegs into round, resurrection holes.

The last alternative, and the one I want to argue for, is *up*—further up and further in. This approach admittedly does not answer or explain what the resurrection will be like exactly, and so it might be frustrating to those who want an advance peek at it. But it does solve the problems by faith. God will not raise us from the dead, male and female, in order to rip us off. The Scriptures invite us to think far above our current material limitations and conditions.

> And if children, then heirs; heirs of God, and joint-heirs with Christ; if so be that we suffer with him, that we may be also glorified together. For I reckon that the sufferings of this present time *are not worthy to be compared* with the

glory which shall be revealed in us. For the earnest expectation of the creature waiteth for the *manifestation of the sons of God.* (Rom. 8:17–19)

John says,

Beloved, now are we the sons of God, and *it doth not yet appear what we shall be:* but we know that, when he shall appear, we shall be like him; for we shall see him as he is. And every man that hath this hope in him purifieth himself, even as he is pure. (1 John 3:2)

In this view, *we* do not transcend materiality or sexuality, but our material sexuality does transcend itself, and in doing so becomes *more* like itself, not less. Heaven is glorious maturity, not an infantile regress. Because we cannot imagine this rightly (being infantile now), the Spirit helps us in our weakness.

This means that in the resurrection there will always be a sky above us. There is always room for another glorious invitation to go further up and further in. But if the ideal of heaven is that of a perfect version of our life here, but one that has no death for closure, eternal life seems to me more like a narrow corridor that goes on forever, with a ceiling eight feet high. The problem with our desires, including our sexual desires, is not that they are overpowering, but that they are insipid and weak. Before we can know true desire, we shall have to be raised. Until then we can only imagine and pray. Again Lewis: "Lust is a poor, weak, whimpering, whispering thing compared with that richness and energy of desire which will arise when lust has been killed."

A CHIASTIC CATECHISM ON BIBLICAL SEXUALITY

———————

H ere are twenty-five questions, along with some
suggested answers.

1. What is the first challenge of biblical masculinity?

   To have enough of it to be willing to articulate what it is in public.

2. Is not the subject of human sexuality filled with nuance?

   Yes, it is. And the first sign that you have worked through it with sufficient care is that nobody thinks you have any.

3. I am beset with sexual temptations. Does God have a solution for me?

   Yes. The love of a good woman who is willing to make love to you for the rest of your life.

4. But I am not married. What should I do about sexual temptation in that case?

   You should find out her name, and ask her.

5. What is the best thing I can do for my children?

   On an earthly level, the best thing you can do for your children is to love their mother.

6. What is the next best thing I can do for my children?

   Get a job where you have to work hard, make sure you do in fact work hard, providing their mother with the wherewithal to feed and clothe them, and to provide them all with a godly education.

7. What do I do if I don't understand my wife?

   God didn't tell you to understand her. He said to love her. Try starting with that.

8. Doesn't the apostle Peter say that husbands are to live with their wives with understanding?

   Yes, he does. Mysteries are to be handled with understanding, which is not the same thing as understanding mysteries.

9. What are the most important things I can do to foster family unity?

   Worship together, pray together, eat together, laugh together, and read together.

10. Why are men sexually attracted to other men?

    It is the judgment of God upon our culture because we would not honor God as God and would not give Him thanks.

Therefore God has given men over to the downward spiral of their renegade lusts fueled by father hunger.

11. How did God imprint His image on the human race?

    He did this by creating us male and female. Any attempts to reconfigure this arrangement are therefore explicit assaults on the image of God.

12. What is the most important word in the marriage vows?

    In our time, because of the peculiar form our disobedience has taken, the most important word is obey. *And it is the most important word whether or not it is included in the vows. Like a father who has abandoned his family, that word can dominate through its absence.*

13. What is biblical masculinity?

    It is the glad assumption of sacrificial responsibility.

14. How do I acquire the authority to live like this?

    Authority naturally flows to those who take responsibility. Authority routinely flees those who seek to blame others.

15. What is the confessional issue of our time?

    The confessional issue of our time is human sexuality, biblically defined.

16. Why are women sexually attracted to other women?

    This also is the judgment of God upon our culture, and is the result of men—fathers, brothers, cousins, boyfriends, husbands, and ex-husbands—mistreating girls and women. Women ineffectively try to build a fortress that will protect them from rebellious male sexuality, but it cannot work. Despite this protest, many self-identified lesbians remain sexually accessible to selfish men, and the "burned by men" phenomenon just gets continually worse. This too is fueled by father hunger.

17. What are the most important things I can do to foster marital unity?

    Worship together, pray together, eat together, sleep together, laugh together, and read together.

18. How can I communicate to my wife how hard it is to take this kind of responsibility?

    You shouldn't try. It is more important for you to be a protective father to her than for her to be a comforting mother to you. Your wife should know that you are faithful. She may or may not know how hard it is. If you are not a whiner, you will not make a point of letting her know.

19. What do I do when my wife doesn't understand me?

    She is not supposed to understand you. She is supposed to respect you.

20. What is the second best thing I can do for my wife?

    Dinner for two at Angelo's, followed by a leisurely walk on the beach in the moonlight.

21. What is the best gift I can give my wife?

    On an earthly level, the best gift you can give your wife is to be a true and faithful father to her children.

22. What do I do about remaining sexual temptations, despite the fact that I am married?

    Recognize that you answer to Christ for your sin, and not primarily to your wife. Unrepented sexual sin, including your internal lusts, is a violation of your marriage vows, but it is a more profound violation of your baptism. Deal with it on that level first.

23. So having repented, what do I do about it?

    Recognize that you are not yet devoted to your wife as a complete woman. If she is your wife in the bedroom, but everywhere else is a servant (or dominatrix), you need to confess your overall husbandly neglect of her, and ask God to dismantle the standing wall of partition you have built up between the two of you. Sexual lusts grow on that wall like ivy.

24. What is the great danger sign that preachers and teachers in the church are compromised on the topic of sexuality?

    The great danger sign is carefully-parsed, visible nuance, coupled with an unwillingness to attack sexual sin, particularly the perversions. As Chesterton noted, to be carefully wrong is a distinguishing mark of decadence.

25. All of this is a high challenge. Will I be able to incorporate these truths into my life?

    That is up to you. But even if you do not believe yourself to be enough of a man, you can at least make the effort manfully.